JURASSIC WORLD™

WHERE DINOSAURS COME TO LIFE

Caroline Rowlands

CARLTON KiDS

How to Use this Book

Discover an amazing world with Augmented Reality

This book, together with the free app, uses the very latest Augmented Reality (AR) technology to mix the real and virtual worlds together. Viewed through your mobile device, Jurassic World dinosaurs will appear to come to life as interactive animations.

Wow! What do I need?

To run the Augmented Reality animations, all you need is this book, the app and a mobile device that meets the minimum requirement specification below.

System Requirements
This product works with the following:
- Apple devices using iOS version 4.3 and above, including iPhone 3GS and upwards, iPod Touch 4G and upwards, and iPad 2 and upwards.
- Android devices with two cameras using Android version 4.0 and above, such as the Samsung Galaxy Nexus and the Asus Google Nexus 7 tablet.
- Dual User mode will require an active wi-fi connection.

It's easy! Here's what you need to do...

1 Download the free **iCarltonAR** 'Where Dinosaurs Come to Life' app from www.apple.com/itunes or www.android.com.apps to your mobile device. Open the app and go to the home page.

2 Tap the Jurassic World button to activate the AR and discover 5 Jurassic World dinosaurs. There are 3 modes to choose from: Single User, Dual User and Life-Size.

3 There are 5 dinosaur AR Activation Pages in this book. Select a mode, then hold your mobile device to view any of the Activation Pages to release incredible Augmented Reality dinosaurs!

4 Take photographs of your dinosaurs as they explore your home, tower over your friends or roam with other dinosaurs. The camera button lets you save to your photo album to share later.

Single User

Release a Jurassic World dinosaur into your home by viewing any of the 5 AR Activation Pages in the book through your mobile device!

Step 1 – Select the Single User mode, tap the **Start** button and your camera will automatically activate. View any of the Activation Pages to make the dinosaur appear.

Step 2 – Use the onscreen **joystick control** to make your dinosaur walk around, hear it roar and take a picture of your dinosaur with the camera button.

Once you get used to the controls, try walking your dinosaur off the page and further away. Try out different angles or hold your device up close to see amazing detail.

Dual User

Grab a friend with the app downloaded to a second device to release two Jurassic World dinosaurs and roam together!

Step 1 – Both users should have the app activated in Dual User mode. The first user taps **Start** and views THESE pages (4-5) to activate the AR and select their dinosaur.

Step 2 – The second user then taps **Start** and views these pages from the SAME BOOK to select their dinosaur.

Step 3 – Both users will see TWO dinosaurs on screen, but will only be able to control the dinosaur they selected.

Have fun exploring together, or go off in different directions and see if you can find each other!

Life-Size

Ever wonder how big dinosaurs really were? With this amazing Life-Size mode you can make a Jurassic World dinosaur appear at its real size next to your friend!

Step 1 – Select the Life-Size mode. It's best if you go outside first, or find a very large room!

Step 2 – Put the book on the ground, and make your dinosaur appear as in Single User mode, using one of the AR Activation Pages. Take some steps back and then tap the **zoom button +** on your screen to make your dinosaur grow to its actual life size!

The life-size dinosaurs can't walk, but you can walk around them! Explore the dinosaur from different positions and then get your friends to stand next to them for a truly amazing dinosaur photograph.

5

Isla Nublar

Jurassic World, the world's first fully operational dinosaur theme park, is up and running, finally open to visitors and just waiting to be explored.

DINO TERRITORY

Imagine the world's most incredible adventure holiday ever on an exotic island bursting with prehistoric life. Dinosaur dreams come true for all guests at the luxury destination Jurassic World. Located on Isla Nublar, this is a holiday experience like no other. Visitors get to interact with all kinds of dinosaurs from gentle giants to fierce hunters and learn all about the prehistoric creatures that once ruled the world.

GETTING AROUND

All visitors arrive on the island by ferry, getting their first glimpse of this incredible world class resort from the sea. The ferry docks on Isla Nublar and from there it's a short trip on a high speed monorail to any one of the hotels. Visitors can then easily access the Main Street area of the resort and all of the various shops, restaurants and attractions the park has to offer.

PLAN YOUR VISIT

Even the biggest dinosaur fans should take some time out from the most popular attractions to experience the amazing amenities on offer on Isla Nublar. There's a world class golf course, beautiful botanical gardens and a wild water park. Then, you can come back to relax in one of the resort's luxury hotel rooms at the end of your exciting day.

DID YOU KNOW?

Dinosaurs first appeared around 230 million years ago and ruled our planet for around 160 million years.

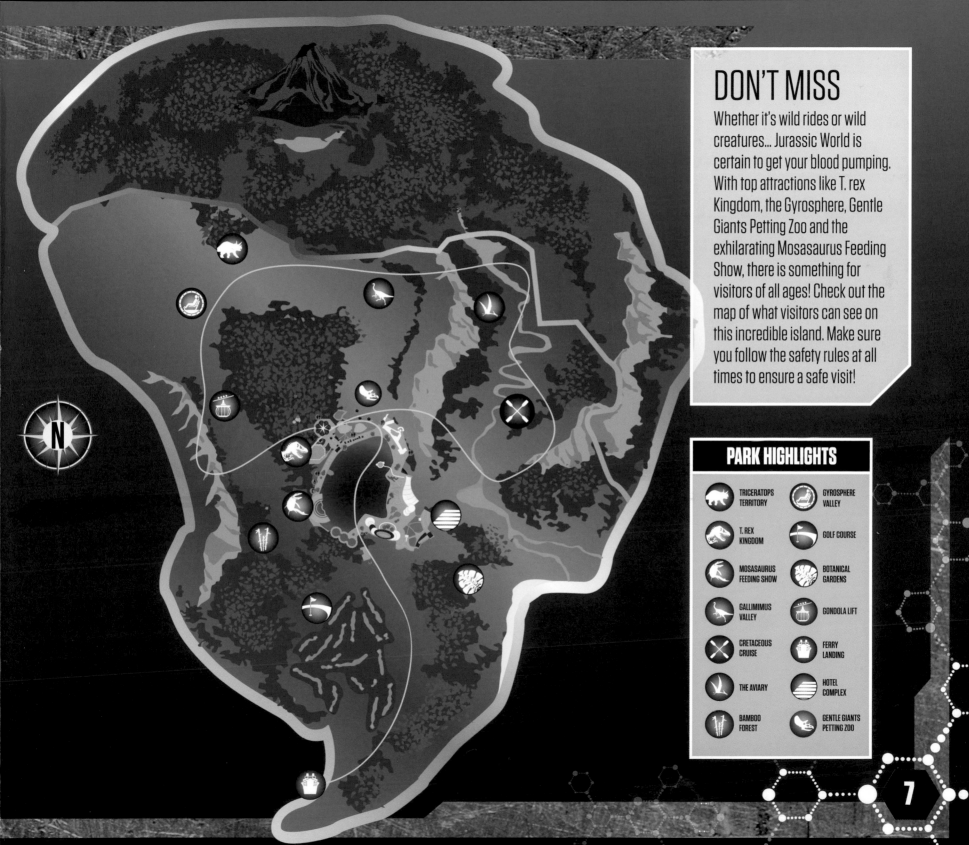

DON'T MISS

Whether it's wild rides or wild creatures... Jurassic World is certain to get your blood pumping. With top attractions like T. rex Kingdom, the Gyrosphere, Gentle Giants Petting Zoo and the exhilarating Mosasaurus Feeding Show, there is something for visitors of all ages! Check out the map of what visitors can see on this incredible island. Make sure you follow the safety rules at all times to ensure a safe visit!

PARK HIGHLIGHTS

TRICERATOPS TERRITORY		GYROSPHERE VALLEY	
T. REX KINGDOM		GOLF COURSE	
MOSASAURUS FEEDING SHOW		BOTANICAL GARDENS	
GALLIMIMUS VALLEY		GONDOLA LIFT	
CRETACEOUS CRUISE		FERRY LANDING	
THE AVIARY		HOTEL COMPLEX	
BAMBOO FOREST		GENTLE GIANTS PETTING ZOO	

N

Jurassic World

Jurassic World includes all kinds of fantastic attractions from the Mosasaurus Feeding Show and Underwater Observatory to T. rex Kingdom and the Gentle Giants Petting Zoo.

PARK'S CENTRE

Located around a beautiful lagoon you can find all the key places for your stay. Relax in one of the luxury rooms, wander along the banks of the lagoon and hop on the monorail to reach the further destinations on the island.

UNDERWATER BEASTS

Millions of years ago, while dinosaurs ruled on land, oceans were filled with incredible prehistoric swimming reptiles. Jurassic World has brought these monsters of the deep back to life.

DID YOU KNOW?

In prehistoric times, mosasaurs probably gave birth to live young at sea.

SCARY SWIMMERS

Jurassic World allows you to see underwater reptiles like the mosasaurs that once filled the oceans and seas. In prehistoric times these huge prehistoric marine reptiles fed on fish, plants and each other.

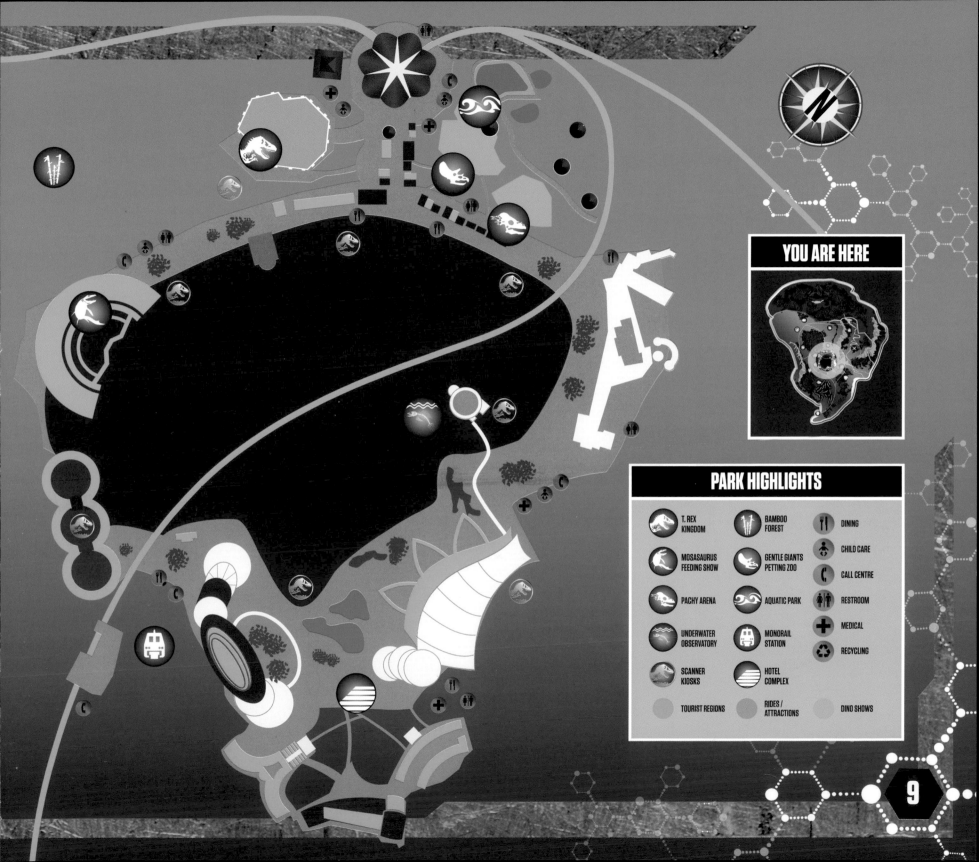

YOU ARE HERE

PARK HIGHLIGHTS

T. REX KINGDOM	BAMBOO FOREST	DINING
MOSASAURUS FEEDING SHOW	GENTLE GIANTS PETTING ZOO	CHILD CARE
PACHY ARENA	AQUATIC PARK	CALL CENTRE
UNDERWATER OBSERVATORY	MONORAIL STATION	RESTROOM
SCANNER KIOSKS	HOTEL COMPLEX	MEDICAL
		RECYCLING
TOURIST REGIONS	RIDES / ATTRACTIONS	DINO SHOWS

9

Valley of the Dinosaurs

Get up close and personal with your favourite dinosaurs using a Gyrosphere, an orb shaped vehicle that allows you to move freely and experience this amazing environment and its creatures at your own pace.

ROAM FREELY

Guaranteed to give goose bumps, the first sighting of these wonderful prehistoric beasts from the safety of the Gyrosphere is one nobody ever forgets. Gyrosphere Valley allows visitors to see dinosaurs eating, sleeping and roaming around in their natural habitats. And the best bit is, for the first time ever, plant-eating dinosaurs from the Jurassic and Cretaceous era exist side by side in this awesome habitat.

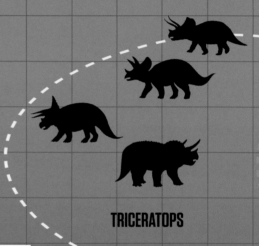

TRICERATOPS

YOU ARE HERE

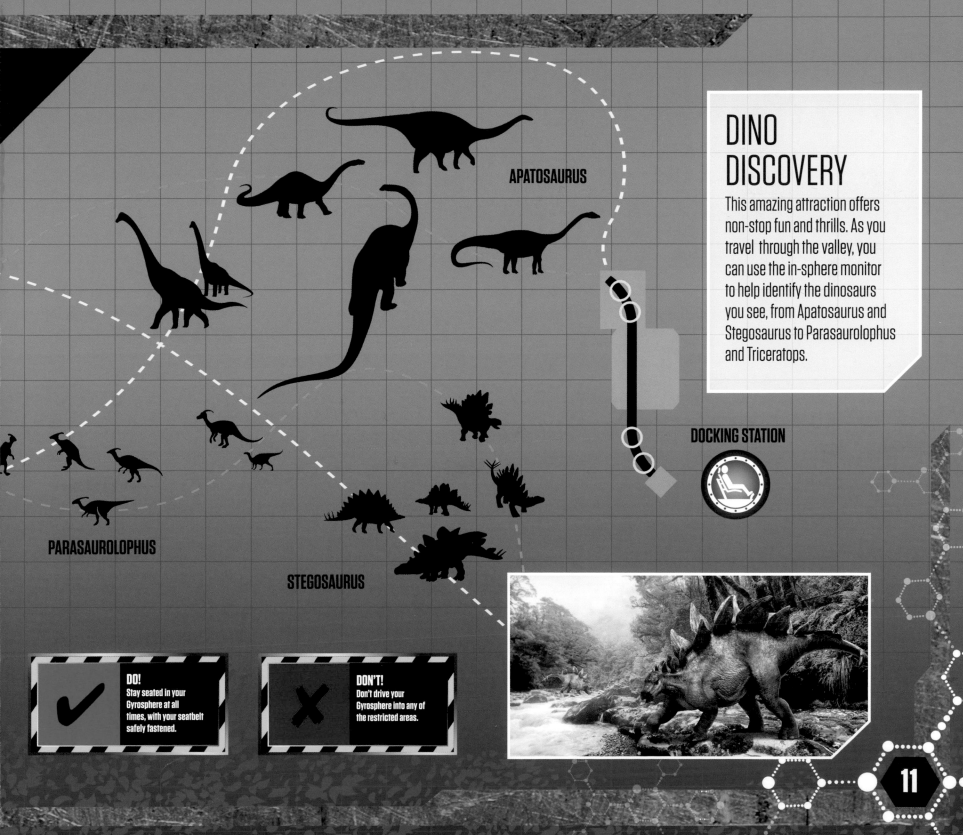

APATOSAURUS

DINO DISCOVERY

This amazing attraction offers non-stop fun and thrills. As you travel through the valley, you can use the in-sphere monitor to help identify the dinosaurs you see, from Apatosaurus and Stegosaurus to Parasaurolophus and Triceratops.

DOCKING STATION

PARASAUROLOPHUS

STEGOSAURUS

DO!
Stay seated in your Gyrosphere at all times, with your seatbelt safely fastened.

DON'T!
Don't drive your Gyrosphere into any of the restricted areas.

Super Science

Dinosaurs that were extinct for millions of years roam, swim and fly, filling all the amazing attractions on this incredible island. But how is it done?

DINO DNA

Technology and science interact in the Jurassic World Creation Lab. Just one drop of blood contains billions of DNA – a blueprint for building a living thing. Millions of years ago when dinosaurs roamed the Earth, mosquitoes were alive as well. After biting a dinosaur, some mosquitoes would get stuck in tree sap, which would eventually fossilize with the mosquito inside. Jurassic World scientists extracted the blood from inside the mosquito and used it to recreate the dinosaur's DNA.

MIRACLE MAKERS

Gene sequencers break down these DNA strands and fill in the holes in the code with that from other animals, such as frogs. Genes are modified and spliced together at the Creation Lab to bring dinosaurs back to life and create new, exciting and deadly breeds.

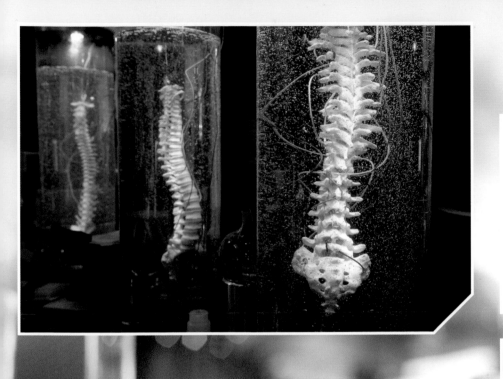

TOP DNA CREATIONS

Every living creature on Isla Nublar, from the vicious Raptors and predatory Pteranodons to the majestic Mosasaurus and terrifying T. rex started out as a DNA blueprint. The brilliant brains at the Creation Lab worked to bring those blueprints to life and revive dinosaurs after 65 million years of extinction.

MESSING WITH NATURE

These daring and evolutionary creations are Jurassic World's biggest achievements. But there is always the danger that the DNA sequencing could get out of control.

T. rex Kingdom

Jurassic World's top attraction T. rex Kingdom is a must for thrill seekers and fans of this most famous and favourite of dinosaurs.

DINO KING

Those brave enough to visit T. rex Kingdom come face to face with a living and breathing legend, and are warned to stay alert. With huge teeth and strong jaw muscles, T. rex is one of the most dangerous predators ever and deserving of its name tyrant lizard king.

FANTASTIC FOSSILS

The first T. rex fossil was discovered by Barnum Brown in 1902. Only around 30 fossils have ever been found, mostly in the United States. Visitors can learn all kinds of fun facts about this prehistoric beast on Isla Nublar, like how a T. rex has around 200 bones – just like us.

TYRANNOSAURUS REX

Say it like this: Tie-ran-o-saw-rus-rex

- **LIVED:** Cretaceous (68 to 66 million years ago) in North America and now, in Jurassic World
- **LENGTH:** 13.4 m long
- **EATS:** meat
- **SPEED:** up to 29 km/h

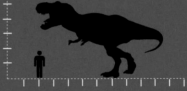

DID YOU KNOW?

T. rex has 50 to 60 teeth in its huge jaw.

BIG BITE

T. rex is a fierce carnivore. This powerful predator can eat up to 230kg of meat in one bite. A T. rex's arms are so short they can't reach its mouth for feeding but the sharp claws on the ends of its arms are useful for stabbing and spearing food.

ACTIVATION PAGE

Release the terrifying **Tyrannosaurus rex** with your mobile device by opening the app and viewing these pages.

Feeding Time

The amazing Mosasaurus Feeding Show at Jurassic World Lagoon is an unforgettable experience for visitors to this incredible island.

MOSASAURUS

Say it like this: Moz-a-saw-rus

- **LIVED:** Cretaceous (70 to 66 million years ago) and now, in Jurassic World
- **LENGTH:** 22 m long
- **EATS:** fish, sharks, birds and other marine life

UNDERWATER GIANT

The fearsome Mosasaurus is a giant member of the family of marine reptiles known as mosasaurs. They are recognizable by their big heads, powerful jaws, streamlined bodies and flippers.

BIG SNAPPER

Crowds cheer as this prehistoric monster of the deep leaps from the water to feed on a Great white shark, dangled as a snack. Back in the Cretaceous period, mosasaurs were the top predators in the sea with their large jaws, stabbing teeth and powerful bite. A hinged jaw allowed them to swallow prey larger than their heads.

THE NEXT GENERATION

For many years, palaeontologists thought prehistoric Mosasaurus went ashore to lay its eggs on land. But after the discovery of a Mosasaurus skeleton with two baby Mosasaurs inside its belly, experts now believe that it had live babies in the water.

POWERFUL PREDATOR

Jurassic World's Mosasaurus is a strong swimmer. It moves through the water in a snake-like way, using its long tail to propel it through the water in search of food. Once caught in Mosasaurus's huge jaws there is no escape.

DID YOU KNOW?

Although it lives in water, Mosasaurus has to rise to the surface to breathe air.

17

Striking Plant-eaters

Once in the beautiful Gyrosphere Valley, one of the easiest dinosaurs to spot is undoubtedly the spikiest star of the show – Stegosaurus.

READY TO DEFEND

Stegosaurus always stands out from the dinosaur crowd thanks to the impressive plates along its back and tail. Experts think they may have helped Stegosaurus control its temperature. On Isla Nublar, Stegosaurus can safely roam with other plant-eating dinosaurs in no fear of attack.

STEGOSAURUS

Say it like this: Steg-o-saw-rus

- **LIVED:** Jurassic (155-145 million years ago) in USA, Europe and possibly China and now, in Jurassic World
- **LENGTH:** 10 m long
- **EATS:** plants
- **SPEED:** up to 7 km/h

SUPER SURVIVOR

On Isla Nublar, Stegosaurus lives in the Gyrosphere Valley but fossils found in the US, Africa, Europe, India and China show how far this species was able to spread across the world and that it survived in many different climates. The first Stegosaurus fossil was found by Othniel Marsh around 1877. Stegosaurus's name means 'roofed lizard'.

SPIKY WEAPON

At the tip of Stegosaurus's tail are sharp spikes. Back in the Jurassic era these pointy hard stakes would have helped to protect Stegosaurus from predators like Allosaurus who lived at the same time. Dino experts have nicknamed the arrangement of these spikes the 'thagomizer'.

DID YOU KNOW?

A Stegosaurus is about the size of a bus but its brain is tiny – about the size of a walnut.

ACTIVATION PAGE

Release the impressive **Stegosaurus** with your mobile device by opening the app and viewing these pages.

Gentle Giants

Apatosaurus is one of the largest living dinosaurs ever. Visitors flock to see this enormous plant-eater in Gyrosphere Valley and enjoy the amazing spectacle of this super-sized sauropod in action.

TAIL TERROR

Back in the Jurassic era, Apatosaurus's biggest enemy was Allosaurus, the most predatory flesh-eater of the period. But at just 5m tall, the Allosaurus was no match for an Apatosaurus or its strong, long tail, which it used as a whip to help defend itself.

A BIG EATER!

This mammoth dinosaur has a massive appetite and spends most of its time feeding. Its long neck lets it feed on leaves high up in trees but it doesn't chew its food. Instead it swallows stones called gastroliths to help grind up the leaves in its stomach.

GROUND SHAKER

Visitors to Gyrosphere Valley, and the other dinosaurs living there, can feel the ground tremble if they get too close to this enormous dinosaur's footsteps. Its huge feet shake the earth beneath, as it stomps through the valley searching for food.

APATOSAURUS

Say it like this: Ah-pat-o-saw-rus

- **LIVED:** Jurassic (154-145 million years ago) in USA and now, in Jurassic World
- **LENGTH:** 27.5 m long
- **EATS:** plants
- **SPEED:** up to 8 km/h

DID YOU KNOW?

Apatosaurus has pencil-like teeth that help it strip leaves from branches.

Dino Defenders

A firm favourite with visitors to the island and famous all over the world, Triceratops gets its name from its three-horned head.

HELPFUL HEAD

A Triceratops' frill of bone around its head helps protect it from the bites of predators. It might also be used to help keep a Triceratops cool, by giving off heat. This dinosaur's small, beak-like mouth snips off ferns and other plants close to the ground. It then shreds the food with rows of sharp teeth.

PERFECT PREY

Back in the Cretaceous era its heavy body and short legs slowed Triceratops down, making it easy to catch for T. rex who lived at the same time. Today Triceratops can roam freely and safely in Jurassic World.

TRICERATOPS

Say it like this: Try-ser-a-tops

- **LIVED:** Cretaceous (68 to 66 million years ago) and now, in Jurassic World
- **LENGTH:** 9 m long
- **EATS:** plants
- **SPEED:** up to 8 km/h

MINI DINOS

Visitors can pet or even ride on the back of a baby Triceratops at the Gentle Giants Petting Zoo. Fossils of Triceratops from prehistoric times are often found together, suggesting that millions of years ago they also lived in herds, with adult Triceratops protecting their young.

DID YOU KNOW?

The first Triceratops skull was found in 1888 by John Bell Hatcher in the USA.

ACTIVATION PAGE

Release the amazing **Triceratops** with your mobile device by opening the app and viewing these pages.

Speedy Hunters

Visitors to Isla Nublar are rewarded with extraordinary sightings of the super-speedy Gallimimus.

DINO DIGGERS

Jurassic World has resurrected this remarkable dinosaur and invites visitors to explore its eating habits and appetite in its natural environment on the Gallimimus Safari. A Gallimimus' long fingers and claws help it dig and grab eggs to eat. As an omnivore, it eats all kinds of food including meat and plants, but has no teeth in its bird-like beak.

DID YOU KNOW?

Gallimimus' name means 'chicken mimic' as it moves like a flightless bird.

GALLIMIMUS

Say it like this: Gall-uh-my-mus

- **LIVED:** Cretaceous (74 to 70 million years ago) in Mongolia and now, in Jurassic World
- **LENGTH:** 4.5 m long
- **EATS:** plants, eggs, insects and lizards
- **SPEED:** up to 40 km/h

4 FUN FACTS

1. Compared to other dinosaurs of its size, Gallimimus has quite a big brain in its small head.

2. A Gallimimus has hollow bones, a bit like a bird's.

3. It is built for speed with long legs, long shins and short toes.

4. Several Gallimimus fossils have been found in Mongolia.

Terror Team

With killer claws, these predators are intelligent, dangerously fast and can communicate with each other, making them the ultimate pack hunters.

DEADLY WEAPONS

Raptors are some of the most vicious and successful predators created in the Creation Lab and living on Isla Nublar. They make up for their small size with the curved killer claws on their feet, which, back in prehistoric times, they used to slash their victims.

VELOCIRAPTOR

Say it like this: Vel-oss-ee-rap-tor

- **LIVED:** Cretaceous (75 to 71 million years ago) in Mongolia and China and now, in Jurassic World
- **LENGTH:** 3.9 m long (and 1.7 m tall)
- **EATS:** meat
- **SPEED:** up to 39 km/h

HUNTING PACK

In prehistoric times, some dinosaurs lived together in groups. Plant-eaters grouped together for protection, and predators like Velociraptors joined forces to hunt in packs and attack much larger dinosaurs.

FIGHT TO THE DEATH

One of the most famous dinosaur fossils ever discovered is called 'Fighting Dinosaurs' and was dug up in Mongolia. It is the fossilized remains of a Protoceratops and Velociraptor, which died together while locked in battle.

ACTIVATION PAGE

Release the ferocious **pack of Raptors** with your mobile device by opening the app and viewing these pages.

Flying High

The amazing creatures on Isla Nublar are not just on land and in the lagoon – swooping pterosaurs soar high in the sky too.

THE AVIARY

With its safe, contained viewing areas, Jurassic World's Aviary is home to all kinds of fantastic flying pterosaurs. From Dimorphodon to Pteranodon, marvel at these gigantic soaring prehistoric reptiles that lived at the same time as the dinosaurs.

FLYING HIGH

Those desiring to catch a glimpse of the Pteranodons and Dimorphodons should plan a visit to the Aviary, where you can safely see these majestic creatures in flight. In prehistoric times these massive flying reptiles would have lived near the sea, flying low and diving into the water to feed on fish and squid.

WINGED WONDER

The Pteranodon was one of the biggest pterosaurs to take to the skies: males had a wingspan of up to 7.6 metres. Its small body and hollow bones meant this huge reptile was light enough to fly. Pteranodon lived during the Cretaceous period.

JURASSIC WORLD
· EST. 1993 ·
PTERANODON PEAK

PTERANODON

Say it like this: Ter-an-o-don

- **LIVED:** Cretaceous (around 88-82 million years ago) in USA and Europe and now, in Jurassic World
- **LENGTH:** 7.6 m wide
- **EATS:** fish

DID YOU KNOW?

The first Dimorphodon fossil was discovered in the UK in 1828 by Mary Anning.

DID YOU KNOW?

Unlike earlier pterosaurs, Pteranodon had a toothless beak, similar to a modern bird's.

29

Untameable

This genetically modified dinosaur was created by Jurassic World's geneticists to be bigger and badder than any dinosaur ever seen before.

BIGGER, LOUDER, MORE TEETH

Created from DNA from the world's fiercest predators, Indominus rex is louder, scarier and has more teeth than any other dinosaur in Jurassic World, or in history.

STAR OF THE SHOW

Indominus rex is the latest dinosaur creation at Jurassic World and one of the most highly anticipated attractions expected to be opening soon. Through careful experiments and studying dinosaurs' characteristics and behaviour, experts in Jurassic World have learned more after a decade of dinosaur genetics than a century of digging up dinosaur fossils.

INDOMINUS REX

Say it like this: In-dom-in-us-rex

- **LIVES:** Now, in Jurassic World
- **LENGTH:** 15.2 m long
- **EATS:** meat
- **SPEED:** up to 45 km/h